ALTERNATOR
BOOKS™

FORCES
AND MOTION

INVESTIGATIONS

KAREN LATCHANA KENNEY

Lerner Publications ◆ Minneapolis

To our future scientists and their unknown discoveries

Content consultant: Kevin Finerghty, adjunct professor of Geology at State University of New York, Oswego; Earth science teacher at Pulaski Academy and Central Schools, Pulaski, New York

Lerner Publications Company
A division of Lerner Publishing Group, Inc.
241 First Avenue North
Minneapolis, MN 55401 USA

For reading levels and more information, look up this title at www.lernerbooks.com.

Main body text set in Aptifer Slab Regular 11.5/18.
Typeface provided by Linotype AG.

Library of Congress Cataloging-in-Publication Data

Names: Kenney, Karen Latchana.
Title: Forces and motion investigations / by Karen Latchana Kenney.
Description: Minneapolis : Lerner Publications, [2018] | Series: Key questions in physical science | Audience: Age 8–12. | Audience: Grade 4 to 6. | Includes bibliographical references and index.
Identifiers: LCCN 2016045747 (print) | LCCN 2016046144 (ebook) | ISBN 9781512440089 (lb : alk. paper) | ISBN 9781512449570 (eb pdf)
Subjects: LCSH: Gravity—Juvenile literature.
Classification: LCC QC178 .K43 2018 (print) | LCC QC178 (ebook) | DDC 531/.11—dc23

LC record available at https://lccn.loc.gov/2016045747

Manufactured in the United States of America
1-42270-26127-3/10/2017

CONTENTS

CHAPTER 3

WHAT MAKES THINGS MOVE?

Gravity is one force that causes motion, but how does motion happen? Newton set out to answer that very question!

BALANCED AND UNBALANCED FORCES

Newton wondered how objects were set into motion. He realized that he could explain how things moved by measuring forces.

A ball flies through the air. But what makes it move and how does it stop?

DIRECTION AND SIZE

What kind of force does it take to score a soccer goal? Every force can be measured in size and direction, and it takes a kick of the right direction and size to score. When you kick a soccer ball toward the goal, which way does it move? That is the kick's direction. You need to kick the soccer ball toward the direction of the goal to score. But it takes more than a kick in the right direction. How far do you need to kick the ball to score a goal? How far the ball travels is the size of the kick's force. Notice that a weaker kick doesn't have a force with a big enough size to go very far. Even a large-size kick in the wrong direction might not earn you a goal. But if you kick the ball with a force of a large enough size that is traveling in the right direction, you can score!

When humans started sending things into space, they had to think carefully about how objects could get there. What would it take to break free of Earth's gravitational pull? Scientists and mathematicians calculated all the forces acting on objects on Earth to figure out just how fast a rocket needs to go to overcome Earth's gravitational pull. The speed you need to overcome gravity is called escape **velocity**. Rockets achieve escape velocity when their powerful engines produce enough force to overcome gravity's downward pull.

To break gravity's hold, a rocket has to quickly reach amazingly fast speeds. It reaches a speed of 7 miles (11 kilometers) per second, which is about 25,000 miles (40,234 km) per hour!

What kinds of forces and motion are at work when you are bouncing on a trampoline?

Rockets use jet forces to accelerate quickly. Forces are what make all kinds of motion possible—from riding your bike to bouncing on a trampoline. Scientists have studied how forces and motion work together on Earth and in space. Their questions—and answers—explain the everyday and extraordinary parts of our world.

You know a lot more about forces and motion now, right? Try this experiment to test how forces affect the motion of a balloon rocket. See if angle affects how fast it speeds along a string. What do you think will happen?

❷ WHAT YOU'LL NEED

- a 10- to 15-foot (3- to 5-meter) piece of kite string
- a plastic straw
- a 6-foot (2 m) ladder
- a 20-foot (6 m) measuring tape
- a long, oval-shaped balloon

- tape
- a watch or clock
- a pencil
- a notebook

❷ WHAT YOU'LL DO

1. Tie one end of the string to a doorknob.
2. Put the other end of the string through the plastic straw.
3. Tie this end of the string tightly to a point on the ladder about 4 feet (1.2 m) from the floor—around the same height as the doorknob.
4. Blow up the balloon, but do not tie it.

5. Hold the end of the balloon tightly while you tape the balloon to the straw. Put the balloon just under the straw. Wrap two pieces of tape over the top of the straw and around the sides of the balloon. Make sure the tape doesn't touch the string.

6. Let go of the end of the balloon, and let the whole balloon move along the string. Observe how it moves. How long does it take before the balloon stops moving? Watch the time and write it down. When the balloon has stopped, measure the distance it traveled and record that information too.

7. Try a second run, but this time, tie the string tightly to the top of the ladder. You may need an adult's help. Pull the balloon back to the ladder, blow it up, and release it again. What happened this time? Record the time it took to travel and the distance it traveled.

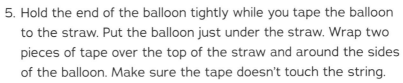 FOLLOW-UP

Review the data from the first and second runs of your balloon rocket. Were the times or distances the same or different? What forces acted to make the rocket move? What can you conclude from your results?

GLOSSARY

acceleration: the measurement of something as it moves faster and faster

air resistance: the force of air pushing against an object's motion, slowing it down

attraction: a pulling force

evidence: information and facts that help prove something is true

friction: a rubbing force that slows down objects

gravity: the force that pulls things toward Earth's surface and which affects all objects with mass

mass: a measure of how much matter, or stuff, is in an object

orbit: the invisible path of an object around a planet or a planet around the sun

resists: pushes away

universe: planets, stars, and all the objects that exist in space

velocity: speed

LERNER

SOURCE™

Expand learning beyond the printed book. Download free, complementary educational resources for this book from our website, www.lerneresource.com.

Idaho Public Television: Gravity Facts
http://idahoptv.org/sciencetrek/topics/gravity/facts.cfm

Kenney, Karen Latchana. *The Science of Race Cars: Studying Forces and Motion*. North Mankato, MN: Checkerboard Library, 2016.

Launchers: How Does a Rocket Work?
https://www.esa.int/esaKIDSen/SEMVVIXJD1E_Liftoff_0.html

Mercer, Bobby. *Junk Drawer Physics: 50 Awesome Experiments That Don't Cost a Thing*. Chicago: Chicago Review, 2014.

NASA: Dynamics of Flight
https://www.grc.nasa.gov/www/k-12/UEET/StudentSite/dynamicsofflight.html

Nova: Galileo's Experiments
http://www.pbs.org/wgbh/nova/physics/galileo-experiments.html

Rowell, Rebecca. *Forces and Motion through Infographics.* Minneapolis: Lerner Publications, 2014.

Swanson, Jennifer. *Explore Forces and Motion! With 25 Great Projects*. White River Junction, VT: Nomad, 2016.

Winterberg, Jenna. *Balanced and Unbalanced Forces*. Huntington Beach, CA: Teacher Created Materials, 2015.

INDEX

PHOTO ACKNOWLEDGMENTS

The images in this book are used with the permission of: design elements: © iStockphoto.com/kotoffei; iDesign/Shutterstock.com. © Allen J. Schaben/Los Angeles Times/Getty Images, p. 4; © Coast-to-Coast/iStock/Thinkstock, p. 5; Brocreative/Shutterstock.com, p. 6; © iStockphoto.com/Difydave, p. 7; © Brand X Pictures/Stockbyte/Thinkstock, p. 8; © Laura Westlund/Independent Picture Service, pp. 9, 17, 21; Georgios Kollidas/Shutterstock.com, p. 10; © iStockphoto.com/IvancoVlad, p. 11; mr.Timmi/Shutterstock.com, p. 12; © iStockphoto.com/traveler1116, p. 13; © iStockphoto.com/dovate, p. 14; NASA/GSFC, p. 15; © iStockphoto.com/thomasmales, p. 16; EHStockphoto/Shutterstock.com, p. 18; matimix/Shutterstock.com, p. 19; © iStockphoto.com/Ohmega1982, p. 20; © Jacek Chabraszewski/Dreamstime.com, p. 22; © Leemage/Universal Images Group/Getty Images, p. 23; © iStockphoto.com/CelsoDiniz, p. 24; NASA/Bill Ingalls, p. 26; Radius Images/Alamy Stock Photo, p. 27.

Front cover: © iStockphoto.com/Aksonov.